WOW!

UNBELIEVABLE FACTS ABOUT
EVERYTHING

PaRragon

Bath · New York · Cologne · Melbourne · Delhi
Hong Kong · Shenzhen · Singapore

50 SUPER SPY facts

John Dee was an astrologer and one of the best-known secret agents for **Queen Elizabeth I**.
#001

He signed any letters he sent to her as 007.
#002

Daniel Defoe, author of *Robinson Crusoe*, was also a spy.
#003

One of America's first spies was soldier **Nathan Hale**.
#004

At the age of 21, he spied on British troop movements in the American Revolutionary War.
#005

He was arrested and executed, but became a hero thanks to his bravery.
#006

Abraham Lincoln created the United States Secret Service in **1865**.
#007

Its main function was to stop people making fake money.
#008

Abraham Lincoln was shot on the day he created the service and died the following day.
#009

It was the first time a US president had been assassinated.
#010

After two more presidents were shot, the Secret Service was assigned to protect the president.
#011

Until **2003**, it was under the charge of the Department of the Treasury.
#012

The British Secret Intelligence Service was formed in **1909**.
#013

Royal Navy Commander **Mansfield Smith-Cumming** and British Army Captain **Vernon Kell** were its leaders.
#014

Their objective during World War I was to find German spies.
#015

During the war, around 120 spies were sent to Britain.
#016

Around 65 of them were caught.
#017

The service is commonly known as MI6 (Military Intelligence, Section 6).
#018

Before he became a famous writer, **Roald Dahl** was a fighter pilot, then worked at the British Embassy in Washington.
#019

MI6 operates alongside the Security Service (MI5).
#020

MI5 deals with threats to national security within the UK.
#021

MI6 deals with threats abroad.
#022

MI6's headquarters are at Vauxhall Cross, in London, England.
#023

MI5 estimates there are as many Russian agents in London today as there were during the Cold War.
#024

The real name of the spy **Mata Hari** was **Margaretha Geertruida Zelle**.
#025

While working as a dancer in France she was arrested for spying for Germany.
#026

At her execution in **1917** she wore a stylish new outfit.
#027

WOW!

UNBELIEVABLE FACTS ABOUT EVERYTHING

This edition published by Parragon Books Ltd in 2016

Parragon Books Ltd
Chartist House
15–17 Trim Street
Bath BA1 1HA, UK
www.parragon.com

ISBN 978-1-4748-5061-2

Printed in China

The escape artist **Harry Houdini** may have been a spy for Britain and the USA. #028

It's believed he passed on information he found out while performing for important kings and rulers around the world. #029

During World War II, some German leaders were suspicious of the UK Scouts – they thought it was a spy movement. #030

The Americans recruited the Mafia to help in the invasion of Italy in World War II. #031

The help that Mafia boss **Lucky Luciano** gave led to his release from prison. #032

The Cambridge Five were British double agents who passed information to Russia during World War II and into the **1950s**. #033

Only four were ever caught – nobody knows who the fifth agent was. #034

Married couple **Julius** and **Ethel Rosenberg** were American Communists executed in **1953** for passing nuclear secrets to the Soviet Union. #035

George Koval was another Soviet spy who stole America's nuclear secrets. #036

It was only discovered he was a spy in **2002**. #037

The Russians once made a lipstick for their agents that was also a gun. #038

A place where secret messages are left is known as a 'drop'. #039

During World War II, the explorer **Jacques Cousteau** posed as a diver in France so he could spy on German naval movements. #042

He received France's Legion of Honour for his efforts. #043

In the **1960s**, the US Central Intelligence Agency (CIA) spent millions of dollars on a spy kit for a cat. #044

The cat would then be able to follow Russian spies without suspicion. #045

Sadly the cat was run over on its first mission. #046

The CIA headquarters is in Virginia, USA. #047

Located there is a museum that only spies can visit. #048

All kinds of amazing gadgets are on display, including a dollar coin that holds microfilm and an underwater spy drone that looks like a catfish, codenamed Charlie. #049

All new CIA agents are given a tour on their first day. #050

Ian Fleming, author of the James Bond books, was a real-life spy. #040 He served in the British Naval Intelligence during World War II. #041

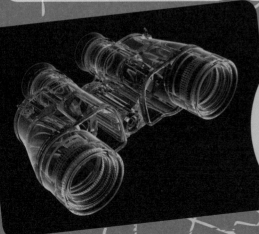

10 FACTS ABOUT GODS AND EMPERORS

The Japanese believe that their emperor is a descendant of **Amaterasu,** the goddess of the Sun and the Universe. #001

The current Japanese emperor, Akihito, is the **125th emperor of Japan.** #002

The Chinese emperor was called the **'Son of Heaven'.** #003

In 331 BC, **Alexander the Great** decided that the Egyptian sky-god, Amun, was his real father! #004

Napoleon Bonaparte became Emperor of France in 1804 – yet he was not even born in France! #005

Napoleon made his **three brothers kings** and his **sister a grand duchess.** #006

The Roman emperor, **Caligula,** went mad and appointed his horse, Incitatus, a priest. #007

Diocletian was the first Roman emperor ever to resign. He retired to a palace in Croatia and grew cabbages there instead. #008

After he died in 44 BC, **Julius Caesar** was officially recognized as a **god** by the Roman State. #009

When **Ogedei Khan** of the Mongol empire died in AD 1241, the Mongol armies fighting in Western Europe had to go home to Asia to elect a new emperor. #010

4 ANCIENT FACTS ABOUT CIVILIZATIONS

Writing **words** using pictures and signs first appeared about **5,500 years ago.** It was another 2,000 years before the first alphabet appeared. `#001`

The world's oldest known scientific **CALCULATOR** was made around **100 BC.** `#002`

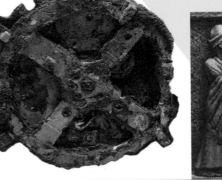

Around 2110 BC, King Ur-Nammu of Ur became the first ruler to **WRITE DOWN THE LAWS OF HIS LAND** in a written code. There were 57 laws. `#003`

Around 500 BC, King Darius, ruler of the Persian Empire, built a **royal road** to a capital city over **2,500 kilometres away.** On foot, the journey would take at least 90 days. `#004`

4 GOLDEN NUGGETS ABOUT ANCIENT GREECE

In the Greek state of **Sparta, boys** were taken from their mothers at seven years old and sent to boot camps, where they were brought up in packs and competed in mock fights. #001

The Ancient Greeks invented the **THEATRE,** building huge amphitheatres for plays. All the actors were men – even those playing women's parts! #002

The Ancient Greeks worshipped **many gods,** including twelve main gods and goddesses who lived on Mount Olympus. #003

At 20, the Spartans were given a **TOUGH FITNESS AND LEADERSHIP TEST** in order to join the military, and their duty didn't end until they were 60. #004

10 FACTS ON THE ANCIENT ROMANS

A Roman **centurion** was in command of 80 men, divided up into ten units of eight men each. #001

The Romans discovered **concrete!** They mixed lime, volcanic ash and water. #002

Boys were **beaten** in Roman schools if they made mistakes! #003

In Ancient Rome, urine was collected, and used for **tanning leather** and **cleaning togas.** #004

The **Pantheon**, a temple to the gods, was built in AD 126. It is still the world's largest unreinforced concrete dome. #005

Roman legions were named after their **qualities** or the **places** they served in. #006

The Romans made **hamburgers** more than 2,000 years ago and ate **take-away food** from local bars. #007

The world's **first fire engine** was invented by the engineer Hero, from Roman Egypt. #008

The Romans heated their houses with the world's **first central heating system,** known as a hypocaust. #009

While everyone else used scythes to cut corn, the Romans developed an early **combine harvester!** #010

5 FASCINATING VIKING FACTS

The name **'VIKING'** comes from a language called Old Norse and means **'A PIRATE RAID'**. #001

Viking **LONGBOATS** were cleverly designed to **FLOAT HIGH** in the water and **LAND ON BEACHES** – so the Vikings could jump out of the ship and join a raid quickly. #002

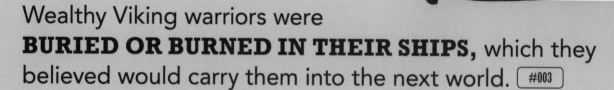

Wealthy Viking warriors were **BURIED OR BURNED IN THEIR SHIPS,** which they believed would carry them into the next world. #003

The word **'BERSERK'** comes from 'Berserkers' – terrifying Viking warriors who wore wolf or bear skins and howled in battle like wild animals. #004

Vikings believed in several gods, including **THOR,** the god of thunder. Our word **THURSDAY** is named after Thor ('Thor's Day'). #005

10 FACTS ABOUT THE WORLD'S BLOODIEST BATTLES

The world's **longest war** lasted for **116 years**. It was between England and France and started in 1337. #001

The world's **shortest war** lasted just **38 minutes**, when a British fleet attacked the island of Zanzibar in 1896. #002

Between **62 and 78 million** people died during World War II (1939–1945). #003

During the Mongol conquests (1207–1472) **17% of the world's population died.** #004

Nearly **2 million** German and Russian soldiers were **killed or wounded** during a battle at Stalingrad (1942–1943). #005

During the Battle of the Somme, on 1 July 1916, around **19,240 soldiers in the British army were killed.** #006

Around **51,000** soldiers died in a **three-day battle** during the American Civil War (1861–1865). #007

Confederate General 'Stonewall' Jackson was mistakenly **killed by his own men.** #008

The **largest naval battle** took place at Salamis in Greece about **2,500 years** ago. #009

The **largest tank and aerial battles** happened at the same time, at Kursk in 1942, between Germans and Russians. #010

10 FACTS ABOUT RUTHLESS RULERS

In 1258, the Mongol army attacked Baghdad and killed at least **200,000 of its 1 million people.** #001

When an Iranian city rebelled against his high taxes in the 1400s, Central Asian conqueror Timur **killed all 70,000 inhabitants.** #002

The Aztecs of Central America **sacrificed humans to satisfy their gods!** #003

In the 1500s, Russian ruler Ivan the Terrible **killed his own son** during an argument. #004

Kaiser Wilhelm II of Germany abdicated in 1918 after almost **10 million soldiers** died during World War I (1914–1918). #005

During **Pol Pot's** rule of Cambodia, between 1975 and 1979, about **2 million** people were killed – a third of the population. #006

In the 540s BC, **King Nabonidus of Babylon** ate **grass** and thought he was a **goat!** #007

When feared dictator **Joseph Stalin** had a stroke in 1953, his ministers and police were too scared to call a doctor for him! #008

Idi Amin, president of Uganda from 1971 to 1979, killed up to 500,000 opponents. #009

In 1976, **President Jean-Bédel Bokassa,** military ruler of the Central African Republic, declared himself **emperor!** #010

5 EXPLORATORY FACTS ABOUT EXPLORERS

The Norwegian explorer **ROALD AMUNDSEN** was the first man to reach the **SOUTH POLE,** in 1911. #001

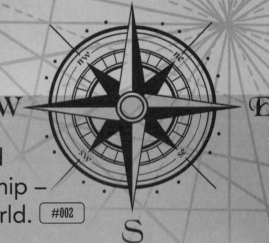

During his lifetime, explorer **IBN BATTUTA** (1304–1368 or 1369) travelled 120,000 kilometres by foot, camel and ship – equivalent to three times around the world. #002

On an expedition in 1862, British explorer **JOHN SPEKE** became temporarily deaf after a **BEETLE** crawled into his ear and he tried to remove it with a knife! #003

In 1860, **ROBERT BURKE** and **WILLIAM WILLS** walked across Australia in search of an **INLAND SEA.** They discovered there was no sea, but then died trying to get home. #004

In 1642, Dutch explorer **ABEL TASMAN** sailed round the whole of **AUSTRALIA** without ever realizing it existed! #005

10 BARMY BLOOD AND BREATHING FACTS

Your **heart** will beat between **2 and 3 billion** times over your lifetime. #001

If you spread all the breathing surfaces inside your lungs out flat, they would be the size of a **tennis court.** #002

With every breath, you take in **air molecules** breathed out by **dinosaurs.** #003

On deep dives without breathing equipment, a diver's lungs shrink to the size of **grapefruits.** #004

Some people who've had a **heart transplant** say they start liking the same food, hobbies and colours as their heart donor. #005

The **heart muscles** squeeze so hard they could squirt blood **10 metres** through the air. #006

Blood is as salty as **seawater.** #007

It takes about **45 seconds** for a blood cell to zoom around the body. #008

Blood cells are made inside your **bones.** #009

Octopuses have **blue blood** and insects have **yellow blood.** #010

10 AMAZING BODY NUMBERS

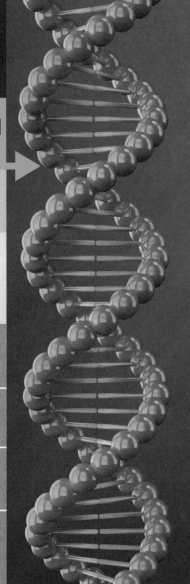

If all the **DNA** in your body was unravelled and stretched out, it could reach to the **Sun and back.** #001

Frenchwoman Jeanne Calment lived to be **122 years old,** older than anyone else on record. #002

A Russian woman, Mrs Vassilyev, is thought to have had **69 children** – 32 twins, 21 triplets and 16 quadruplets. #003

Every human started off as **one cell,** for about the first half an hour that they existed. #004

A sneeze zooms out of your nose and mouth at around **150 kilometres** an hour. #005

Robert Wadlow, the **tallest person ever,** measured **2.72 metres** and had **size 36 feet.** #006

Lucia Zarate, the **smallest person ever**, was **51 centimetres** tall and weighed 2.1 kilograms. #007

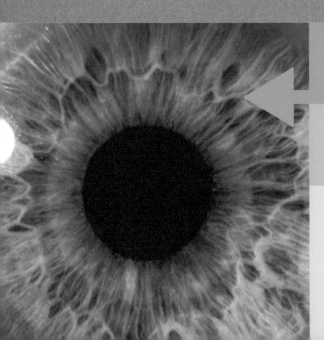

The **human eye** can see stars that are **millions of miles away.** #008

Park ranger **Roy Sullivan** survived being struck by lightning **seven times.** #009

Charles Osborne of Iowa, USA, **hiccupped** non-stop for 68 years. #010

35 RANDOM
BODY FACTS

If all the **blood vessels** in your body were laid out in a line they would reach **twice around the world.** #001

Human bone is **stronger than concrete or steel.** #002

You have over **200 bones** in your body. #003

Over half of all the bones in your body are in your **feet and hands.** #004

People used to **drill holes in skulls** to cure headaches. #005

The ancient Aztecs used **human thighbones to make musical instruments.** #006

The body rots away after death, but **bones can last for thousands of years.** #007

After the age of about 30, people's **skeletons start to shrink.** #008

The **smallest bone** in your body is in your **ear** and is 0.3 cm long. #009

Bones can repair themselves if they get broken, but teeth can't. #010

Your **funny bone isn't a bone**, but a sensitive nerve running past your elbow joint. #011

Some snores are as loud as a road drill. #012

You spend around **a third of your life** asleep. #013

When you dream, you don't **invent people's faces** – they are people you've seen before. #014

The record for a human lasting without sleep is **18 days, 21 hours and 40 minutes.** #015

An Italian man named Francesco Lentini had **three legs.** #016

People can have **artificial** legs, arms, feet, noses, hearts, hips, teeth, ears and hands. #017

Weird things have been found **inside people's stomachs,** including...

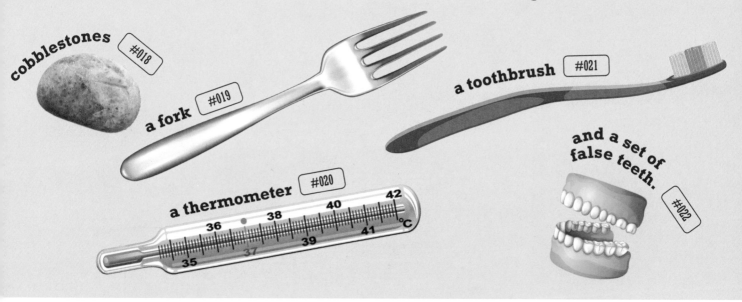

cobblestones #018

a fork #019

a thermometer #020

a toothbrush #021

and a set of false teeth. #022

You are **taller in the morning** because gravity squashes your body slightly during the day. #023

Your fingers have **no muscles.** They are **controlled by muscles in your arms.** #024

Some people have **five fingers and one thumb** on each hand. #025

If you **stretch your arms wide,** the distance between your fingertips **is the same as your height.** #026

Doctors have mistakenly **left things inside people's bodies** after surgery, including a **needle** #027 , **scissors** #028 , **tweezers** #029 , **pliers** #030 and **a sponge.** #031

The human body contains around **75 trillion cells.** #032

A typical human cell is **10 microns across** – about the size of a single speck of talcum powder. #033

The **longest cells** in the human body are **nerve cells** that reach from the toes to the spine. #034

In the time it takes you to read this sentence, **30 million** of your cells have **died and been replaced.** #035

5 DEADLY ANIMALS

HIPPOS kill more people every year than sharks, bears, lions or leopards. #001

A **GOLDEN POISON DART FROG** is so poisonous that you could die from just touching it. #002

You can tell when a **BLUE-RINGED OCTOPUS** is about to deliver a **DEADLY BITE** – bright blue rings suddenly appear all over its body. #003

The **BOX JELLYFISH,** the most venomous creature on Earth, is almost invisible in water. #004

NEEDLEFISH sometimes leap out of the water and accidentally stab fishermen with their **SHARP SNOUTS.** #005

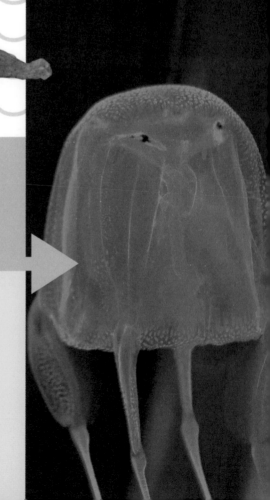

The **flying fox** isn't a fox – it's a **giant bat,** with wings that can be almost **2 metres** across. #001

Bar-headed geese fly over the Himalayas at up to **8,000 metres** – almost as high as Mount Everest. #002

Hummingbirds can beat their wings so fast that they appear **invisible.** #003

The wandering albatross can have a **3.5-metre wingspan,** so each wing is as long as an adult human. #004

Flying fish use their fins as wings to glide up to **180 metres** through the air. #005

To **fly like a bird,** we would need wings as big as dinner tables! #006

One type of tiny **midge** can beat its wings more than **1,000 times every second.** #007

The **longest recorded flight** by a **chicken** is **13 seconds.** It flew just over 100 metres. #008

A **swarm of flying locusts** can contain **10 billion** insects and be so thick it blocks out the sunlight. #009

In 1973, a **Rüppell's vulture** flew into an aircraft at an altitude of **11,000 metres** – the highest bird flight ever recorded. #010

10 CREEPY FACTS ABOUT SEA CRITTERS

The **lion's mane jellyfish** can have tentacles **30 metres** long. #001

A **sea cucumber** can excrete its internal organs to reduce in size! #002

When a **pistol shrimp** snaps its claw, it makes a noise as loud as a jet engine and heats the water nearby to **4000°C.** #003

One single **hagfish** can turn a whole bucket of water into **slime** in minutes by releasing horrible mucus from its body. #004

The **dresser crab** wears **camouflage.** It covers itself with bits of seaweed, sponges and other sea creatures. #005

All **clownfish** are born **male,** but some later change into **females.** #006

The **barreleye fish** has a see-through head, with its eyeballs buried deep inside it. It looks through its own head to see! #007

To eat, **starfish** turn their **stomach inside out** and wrap it around their food. #008

Handfish walk on the seabed with fins that **work like legs.** #009

The **deep-sea giant isopod** looks like a **woodlouse,** but is much bigger! #010

5 AWESOME OCTOPUS FACTS

The **MIMIC OCTOPUS** can imitate the shape of a flatfish, a jellyfish, a stingray, a seahorse or a deadly sea snake. #001

An octopus has **THREE HEARTS** and **NINE BRAINS** – one main brain and a smaller one for each of its tentacles. #002

Octopuses can change **SHAPE, COLOUR AND TEXTURE,** so they can pretend to be a speckled rock, bumpy coral or frilly seaweed. #003

The deep-sea **DUMBO OCTOPUS** is like the cartoon elephant because it has massive flappy 'ears' (which are actually fins). #004

An octopus can distract predators by squirting an **INK CLOUD** that creates an octopus-like shape. #005

33 CRAZY CULTURAL FACTS

Nine countries in the world have **nuclear weapons.** #001

15 countries, including Costa Rica, have **no military forces.** #002

There are about **1.4 million men and women** on active duty in the US military. #003

Russia is the **largest country,** covering over 17 million square kilometres, or **13% of the world's land area.** #004

The world's smallest country is the **Vatican City in Rome.** It covers 0.44 square kilometres, or around 62 football pitches. #005

The coral islands of the Maldives in the Indian Ocean peek out of the sea at a **maximum height** of **2.4 metres.** #006

Tibet is the **highest region** in the world, at a height of 4,900 metres above sea level. #007

The border between Canada and the United States is the **longest international border** between two countries, at **8,891 kilometres.** #008

Most countries have a coastline, but **48 are landlocked**, which means citizens have to pass through another country to get to the sea. #009

Nearly 18,000 people pack into every square kilometre of the principality of Monaco, the world's **most densely populated country.** #010

There are only **1.7 people for every square kilometre** of Mongolia, the world's emptiest country. #011

Japan has the oldest population, with nearly a quarter of people aged over 65. #012

The Burj Khalifa building in Dubai is nearly 830 metres tall, or **as tall as 100 stacked houses.** #013

Disabled athletes have a long history of competing in the Olympic Games. An American gymnast competed in 1904 with one leg, and a one-armed Hungarian took part in shooting events in 1948 and 1952. #014

The UK pound sterling is the **oldest currency still in use.** The silver penny was introduced around 1,300 years ago. #015

Paper money was first used in China in 1024. #016

It is believed that the **first coins** were produced in Aegina in Greece in around **700 BC.** #017

In 1946 the Hungarian national bank issued a banknote for **100 quintillion (100 million million million)** pengo. #018

Somalia issued a coin **in the shape of a guitar.** #019

There are **150 billion US 1 cent coins** in circulation. #020

If all the US 1 cent coins in circulation were piled up they would stand **232,500 kilometres** high, or three-fifths of the way to the Moon. #021

Each US 1 cent coin loses money, as they cost **2.4 cents to make** and distribute. #022

If you counted one US 1 cent coin every second it would take **4,757 years to complete counting.** #023

Some people have unusual beauty rituals including **teeth sharpening, ear elongations, nose studs and lip plates.** #024

The **world's oldest international organization** was set up in Britain in 1839 to campaign for the abolition of slavery. It is now called Anti-Slavery International. #025

The United Nations was formed in 1945 to promote **world peace**. It has **193 members.** #026

The **Red Cross** was set up in 1863 after a Swiss businessman witnessed the wounded lying on a battlefield and was appalled at the lack of medical care. #027

The idea for the **Scouts** came during a war in South Africa in 1899–1902. **Robert Baden-Powell** was so impressed with the young cadets who ran errands that he founded the Scouts when he got home. #028

The **Academy Award Oscar** statue is modelled on Mexican film director and actor Emilio Fernandez. #029

James Cameron directed the two highest-earning movies of all time, *Avatar* and *Titanic*. Combined, they have made over **£2 billion at the box office.** #030

If the figures for the highest-earning film were adjusted to allow for price rises since release, *Gone With the Wind* from 1939 would be **the most successful.** #031

The longest film ever made is *Modern Times Forever*, which runs for **10 days.** #032

The **first feature film with dialogue and music** was *The Jazz Singer*, a 1927 musical. #033

10 LUDICROUS FACTS ABOUT LAWS

In the UK, it's an **act of treason** to place a postage stamp of the Queen's head upside down. #001

In France, it is forbidden to call a pig **Napoleon.** #002

In Singapore, **chewing gum** is banned. #003

In Florida in the USA, it is illegal to **skateboard** in a police station. #004

In the UK, the head of any **dead whale** found on the coast is legally the property of the king; the tail belongs to the queen. #005

In London, it is illegal to **flag down a taxi** if you have the **plague.** #006

In Alabama in the USA, it's illegal to be **blindfolded** while driving a vehicle. #007

In Eraclea in Italy, it is forbidden to build **sandcastles.** #008

In Vermont in the USA, women must obtain written permission from their husbands to wear **false teeth.** #009

In Switzerland, it's illegal to **flush a toilet** in a flat after 10pm. #010

10 SPORTING FACTS TO EXERCISE YOUR BRAIN

The **oldest sporting event** is the Newmarket Town Plate horse race, run almost every year since 1665. #001

The **most popular sport** is football. Around 3.3 billion people watch or play the game. #002

The **biggest ever football crowd,** of nearly 200,000 fans, watched the World Cup final between Brazil and Uruguay in Rio de Janeiro in 1950. #003

The World Cup football competition has been held **19 times** since it started in 1930. #004

More than **2 million people** lined the streets of Madrid to welcome home the winning Spanish World Cup football team in 2010. #005

Around **15 million people** watch the Tour de France cycle race each year. #006

Up to **400,000 people** watch the annual Indianapolis 500 motor race in the USA. #007

Formula 1 racing cars can reach speeds of up to **350 kilometres per hour!** #008

In 1661, the **first yacht race** took place on the River Thames between King Charles II and his brother, the Duke of York. #009

Ever since 2000, competitors have taken part in the annual **Mobile Phone Throwing** World Championship! #010

10 TERRIFIC TRANSPORT FACTS

A **Boeing 747** travels **800 metres** on each litre of fuel. As it can carry 550 passengers, it's more fuel efficient than most cars. #001

Early airships were filled with hydrogen, a highly flammable gas. After some deadly explosions, helium was used instead. #002

The **longest train** in the world was 7,350 metres long. It had eight engines and 682 wagons! #003

The **earliest known successful flight** was by hot air balloon in Paris in 1783. #004

The word **'juggernaut',** a huge lorry, is Indian – it's the name of a Hindu temple cart said to be used to crush people. #005

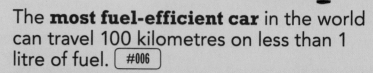

The **most fuel-efficient car** in the world can travel 100 kilometres on less than 1 litre of fuel. #006

Maglev trains have **no wheels** – they are suspended above a rail by magnetic force. #007

In 1972, Jean Boulet landed a helicopter safely after the **engine failed** at a height of 12,440 metres. #008

The South American Aztecs didn't make use of the **wheel,** so didn't have carts or carriages. Instead they travelled and transported things via canoe. #009

There will be around **200,000** aeroplane flights in the world today. #010

10 MIND-BENDING FACTS ABOUT GOVERNMENTS

Elizabeth II of the UK is also queen of **16 Commonwealth countries,** including Canada, Australia, New Zealand and Jamaica. #001

The current **longest-serving head of state,** King Rama IX of Thailand, has been in power since 1946. #002

The current **oldest head of state** is Robert Mugabe, who was born in 1924. #003

No king or queen has entered the **UK House of Commons** since 1642... #004

... when Charles I stormed in with his soldiers and **tried to arrest** five members of Parliament. #005

Of all the countries in the world, 44 are monarchies, including 16 Commonwealth nations. #006

The **biggest democracy** in the world is India. **714 million people** were eligible to vote in the Indian general election of 2009. #007

A **theocracy** is a system of government based on religion – the head of state is selected by a religious group. #008

There are two theocracies – the **Vatican City** in Rome, home of the Roman Catholic Church, and **Iran,** an Islamic republic. #009

In **Australia** it is compulsory for citizens over the age of 18 to vote. #010

27

10 POPULAR FACTS ABOUT POPULATIONS

The world's **population** is over **7 billion** and rising fast. #001

In **1960,** the population of the world was **3 billion** people. #002

During 2011, about **135 million** people were born in the world... #003

The world's population is increasing by **2.4 people a second.** #004

... and **57 million** died. That's an increase of 78 million people in just one year. #005

252 babies are born in the world every minute, or **4.2 births a second.** #006

107 people die in the world every minute, or **1.8 deaths a second.** #007

The highest life expectancy in the world is in Japan – **83 years.** #008

More than **60%** of the world's population live in **Asia.** #009

On 29 May 2007, for the first time in human history, more people lived in **cities and towns** than in the countryside! #010

10 TONGUE-TWISTING FACTS ON LANGUAGES

The most commonly spoken language in the world is **Mandarin Chinese,** spoken by **845 million people.** #001

The United Nations recognizes **six official world languages:** Mandarin Chinese, Spanish, English, Arabic, Russian and French. #002

Around the world, people speak about **6,500 different languages.** #003

Approximately 83 of these are spoken by **80% of the world's population**. #004

Approximately 473 of the world's languages are **almost extinct** and spoken only by a few people. #005

Approximately one language dies out in the world **every two weeks,** when its last speaker dies. #006

The **Sumerian language** of the Middle East is one of the earliest on record, dating back to around **2900 BC**. #007

Most **European languages** are closely related to each other, such as German and Dutch. #008

However, **Euskara,** the language of the Basque people in northern Spain, is **unrelated to any other known language** in the world. #009

In 1825, blind Frenchman **Louis Braille** developed a language that could be read by blind people by feeling a series of bumps on paper. #010

50 facts about WONDERS

The **Salar de Uyuni** in Bolivia is the world's largest salt flat. `#001` It covers an area of around 10,500 km². `#002` Once a lake, the water evaporated and left a thick salt crust. `#003` The flat white landscape causes optical illusions and reflects colours. `#004` Locals have built hotels made entirely of salt for tourists. `#005`

The **Ngorongoro Crater** in Africa was created when a huge volcano exploded 2–3 million years ago. `#006` The 300 km² area is home to around 25,000 animals including lions, rhinos and leopards. `#007`

Uluru, or **Ayers Rock**, in Australia, is 348 m high and over 9 km in circumference. `#008` The rock is a sacred place for the Aboriginal people who have lived there for thousands of years. `#009` It's around 600 million years old and would have originally sat at the bottom of the sea. `#010` Its orange colour is caused by the oxidation of the iron in the rock. `#011`

The highest uninterrupted waterfall in the world is **Angel Falls** in Venezuela. `#012` The waterfall has a height of 979 m. `#013` That's nearly 20 times taller than Niagara Falls. `#014` It is named after Jimmie Angel, an aviator from the United States. `#015` He was the first person to fly over the falls, in 1930. `#016`

The **Grand Canyon** is 433 km in length. `#017` At its widest point it stretches 29 km across. `#018` It is around 1,800 m deep. `#019` The Colorado River runs through the canyon. `#020` The rock found at the bottom of the canyon is around 2 billion years old. `#021` It became a National Park in 1919. `#022` Almost 5 million people visit every year. `#023`

The aurora borealis, or **northern lights**, is an amazing natural light display that can be seen from areas near the North Pole. #024 The lights are caused by charged particles that come from the Sun and hit air molecules in the upper atmosphere. #025 We are usually protected from these particles by Earth's magnetic field, but there are weak spots near the polar regions. #026 In these areas, the charged particles react with particles in the air and become visible. #027

One of the world's largest bays is the **Guanabara Bay** in Brazil. #028 It measures 28 km from east to west. #029 It is 30 km from north to south. #030 It has 80 km of beaches. #031 Within the harbour are around 130 islands. #032 The bay is surrounded by tall granite mountains. #033 On top of Corcovado is a statue of Jesus Christ. #034 The statue is almost 40 m tall. #035

The **Great Barrier Reef** is the largest coral reef system in the world. #036 It is 2,300 km long. #037 It covers an area larger than Italy. #038 Astronauts can see it from space. #039 Two million people visit every year. #040

The **Galápagos Islands** in the Pacific Ocean span the equator. #041 They are an offshore territory of Ecuador and are over 900 km from its coast. #042 There are 18 main islands, 3 smaller ones and 107 islets or rocks. #043 The largest island is Isabela. #044 The oldest island is more than 4 million years old. #045 The younger islands are still being formed. #046 Over 25,000 people live there. #047 There are a huge number of endemic species on the island (that only live there), including the marine iguana, flightless cormorant, blue-footed booby and the Galápagos tortoises the island is named after. #048 These giant tortoises have slightly different features, depending on which island they live on. #049 **Charles Darwin** visited in **1835** and his findings there helped him come up with his theory of evolution. #050

10 HURRICANE AND TORNADO FACTS TO BLOW YOUR MIND

Hurricanes are huge spinning storms with winds of over **120 kilometres per hour!** #001

Tornadoes are much smaller than hurricanes, but with winds **three times as strong.** #002

Hurricanes spin **clockwise** south of the equator and **anti-clockwise** north of the equator. #003

A tornado in Italy sucked a **baby** out of his pram, carried him **90 metres** and set him down safely. #004

A tornado in England plucked all the **feathers** off hens in a coop. #005

Waterspouts whipped up by hurricanes at sea can tower over **100 metres.** #006

In 1928, a hurricane dumped over **2.5 billion tonnes of seawater** on the Caribbean island of Puerto Rico. #007

In 1992, a hurricane shifted a **whole island** closer to the US coast! #008

A hurricane unleashes the same amount of energy as a **nuclear bomb.** #009

A US tornado lifted a **train off the tracks** and dumped it **25 metres** away. #010

The **world's deadliest earthquake** hit central China in 1556, killing 830,000 people. #001

Nine out of ten earthquakes strike around the shores of the Pacific Ocean. #002

Tsunamis (giant waves set off by earthquakes) can race across the ocean at **600 kilometres** per hour. #003

In 1755, the Portuguese city of **Lisbon** was totally destroyed by an earthquake, fire and tidal waves. #004

In 1896, Japanese sailors out at sea hardly noticed a tsunami that went on to kill **28,000 people** on land. #005

The Indonesian earthquake of 2004 released **more energy** than all of the earthquakes in the previous five years combined. #006

Often, before a tsunami strikes, all the **water drains away** from the shore, exposing the seabed. #007

An earthquake in 1812 was so strong, it caused the Mississippi River to **flow backwards.** #008

In 1985, a **healthy baby** was found in a ruined hospital in Mexico City seven days after an earthquake destroyed the city. #009

In 1976, scientists noticed animals behaving oddly in a Chinese city. The city was **evacuated** and two hours later an earthquake struck. #010

10 GROUNDBREAKING EARTHQUAKE AND TSUNAMI FACTS

5 DRAMATIC FACTS ABOUT DESERTS

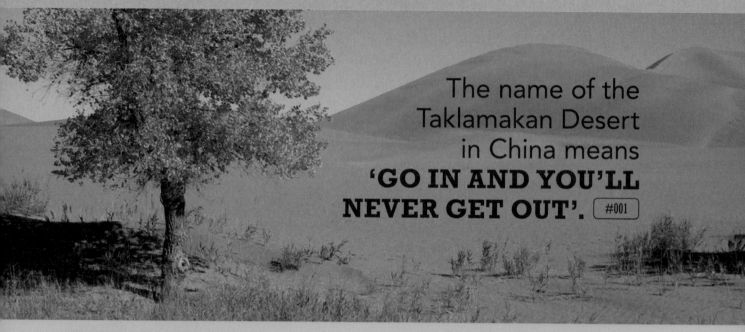

The name of the Taklamakan Desert in China means **'GO IN AND YOU'LL NEVER GET OUT'.** #001

The Sahara Desert, **EARTH'S BIGGEST DESERT,** covers an area about the size of the United States. #002

It is still getting bigger – growing **50 KILOMETRES** south every year. #003

Despite being covered in ice, **ANTARCTICA** is actually classed as a desert because it hardly ever snows! #004

In 1913, the temperature at Furnace Creek in Death Valley, USA, hit a sizzling **56°C** – the highest on record in the country. #005

10 LAVA-LICIOUS FACTS ABOUT VOLCANOES

In 1815, the eruption of **Mount Tambora** in Indonesia spread an ash cloud around the world. #001

Llullaillaco in the Atacama Desert is the **tallest active volcano in the world,** at 6,739 metres! #002

In 1943, a new volcano in Mexico reached **five storeys high in a week** – Mount Paricutin is now 2,800 metres tall. #003

The eruption of **Vesuvius** in Italy in AD 79 perfectly preserved the Roman city of Pompeii under a layer of ash – it lay buried for 1,700 years. #004

Red-hot **lava** flows like sticky liquid. #005

An eruption on the Caribbean island of Martinique in 1902 killed **almost everyone in the island's capital** – only a few survived. #007

Over 60% of all volcanoes erupt **underwater.** #006

Mauna Loa on Hawaii has erupted roughly **every six years since** 1000 BC. #008

In 1985, an eruption in South America buried the town of Armero under **5 metres of mud.** #009

In 1952, a Japanese ship, the *Kaiyo Maru*, sank when an **undersea volcano** erupted just below it. #010

The Atlantic Ocean is getting **4 centimetres wider each year!** #001

The Mariana Trench in the Pacific is **Earth's deepest point** – so deep, it could submerge Mount Everest. #002

The Pacific is Earth's deepest ocean, with an average depth of **4,200 metres.** #003

The Pacific Ocean has more than **25,000 islands.** #004

Seawater freezes at a **lower temperature** than freshwater, at -1.9°C. #005

In 1933, a US Navy ship caught in a Pacific storm survived a **34-metre high wave** – the biggest wave ever recorded at sea. #006

The world's **longest mountain range** is called the mid-ocean ridge – it spans 65,000 kilometres around the globe. #007

The water in a wave doesn't travel forwards like you might think; it goes **round in a circle.** #008

If you could remove all the **salt** from the oceans, it would cover Earth's dry land to a depth of **1.5 metres.** #009

In 1900, 6,000 people died when the town of **Galveston, USA,** was swamped by waves. #010

3 GOBSMACKING ENVIRONMENTAL FACTS

Recycling one aluminium can can save enough electricity to power a TV for three hours and aluminium cans can be recycled an unlimited number of times. #001

At least **20 million hectares of rainforest** are lost every year, which is as big as England, Scotland and Wales combined. #002

The **next ice age** is due to start in about 1,500 years, but might be delayed by climate change. #003

35 FACTS ABOUT
SCIENCE & TECHNOLOGY

Electricity travels as fast as the speed of light, about **300,000 kilometres per second.** #001

One 60-watt light bulb is the equivalent of about **25,000 fireflies.** #002

An electric eel can produce an **electric shock** of 500 volts – enough to kill an adult. #003

Gregor Mendel, a scientist in the 1800s, came up with ideas on **genetics** (how traits are passed from one generation to the next) by looking at **pea pods and their flowers.** #004

The **smallest flowering plant** is *Wolffia angusta*. It would fit inside this letter 'o'. #005

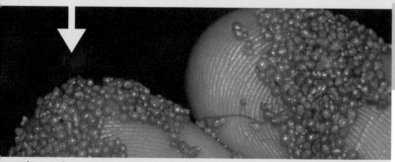

The 'desert onion' onyanga grows in the Namib Desert in Angola. It can live for up to **2,000 years.** #006

A mushroom called 'Lady in the veil' can be heard **cracking as it grows** by a centimetre a minute. #007

African bugleweed contains a chemical that messes up caterpillars so they turn into **butterflies with two heads.** #008

The largest unit of measurement for dista is a **gigaparsec**, about **3.26 billion light years** or **31,000 trillion kilometres.** #009

The **Scoville heat unit (SHU)** is used to measure the **heat of chillies.** #010

Horsepower is used to measure the **power of engines.** It began when people running steam-powered vehicles paid a fee based on the number of horses they had been saved from using. #011

The **number of atoms** in the whole universe is thought to be around 10^{80}. This is **1 followed by 80 zeros.** #012

Most of every atom is **empty space.** Each atom has a **nucleus with electrons whizzi around it** – if the nucleus was the size of a basketball, the electrons would be **32 kilometres away.** #013

If you took all the **space out of atoms**, the whole human race would be **the size of a sugar cube.** #014

Atoms are very tiny – about **25,000,000,000,000,000,000,000 carbon atoms** make up the lead of a pencil. #015

The **oldest known rock** is in Canada and is **4 billion** years old. #016

There are **bacteria that live in the spaces between crystals** inside rocks. #017

Sound travels **ten times faster** through rock than air. #018

Although **rubies are red and sapphires are blue**, they are the same rock – impurities make them **different colours**. #019

The temperature at the Earth's core is **over 5,500°C.** #020

The **magnetic field** of the Earth reverses **four or five times every million years**, with the North and South Poles swapping over. #021

Scientists collect ice up to **800,000 years old** in Antarctica and from bubbles in it they can **sample the ancient atmosphere.** #022

India was once an island and the Himalayas formed when it slowly crashed into Asia, **pushing the edges of each landmass upwards.** #023

Fossils of marine animals are found on Mount Everest and in the Himalayas, as the land that forms them was **once under the sea.** #024

Since 1977 the unmanned **spaceships Voyagers 1 and 2** have been carrying a message for any **aliens they meet.** #025

The USSR put an **unmanned lander on Venus** in 1970. The USA has still not landed a craft on the planet. #026

The temperature on the surface of the Sun is over **5,500°C.** #027

If you could convert the heat energy from a space shuttle's rocket boosters to electric power, **two minutes would supply the power needed by 87,000 homes** for a day. #028

The spacecraft **Rosetta weighed 100 kilograms on Earth**, but when it landed on a comet low gravity **reduced its weight to that of a sheet of paper.** #029

There are 170,000 kilograms of **human junk on the Moon**, including **two golf balls** left by an astronaut. #030

Americans make up **5% of the world's population** but use **25% of the world's energy.** #031

A beam of sunlight usually appears **white**, but is actually made up of different colours. If the beam hits raindrops at the right angle, **the colours separate and we see them as a rainbow.** #032

The iceberg that sank the *Titanic* was made from snow that fell over Greenland **3,000 years ago.** #033

A microbe known as **'strain 121'** lives in holes under the sea that pour out water at **temperatures of 121°C** – much hotter than boiling water. #034

Nothing can be colder than **zero Kelvin (-273°C).** #035

10 SHINING FACTS ABOUT THE MOON

Human footprints on the Moon will last for **millions of years,** because there is no wind to blow them away. #001

The largest crater on the Moon is the South Pole–Aitken basin, almost **2,414 kilometres across!** #002

There are **no noises on the Moon,** because there is no air to carry sounds. #003

As there was no wind, the American flag planted on the Moon by astronauts was **held straight with wire.** #004

Only **12 people** have walked on the surface of the Moon. No one has been there since 1972. #005

The Moon is moving away from Earth at the rate of **3 centimetres a year.** #006

Moonlight takes **1.25 seconds** to reach Earth. #007

We only ever see **one side of the Moon** from Earth. #008

Temperatures on the dark side of the Moon fall to **-173°C!** #009

Most scientists believe the Moon formed when a **collision** broke off a chunk of Earth. #010

5 HOT FACTS ABOUT THE SUN

Sunlight takes **EIGHT AND A HALF MINUTES** to reach Earth, travelling at 300,000 kilometres per second. #001

Fountains of flame **LARGER THAN EARTH** shoot from the surface of the Sun. #002

Dark spots on the Sun called **SUNSPOTS** can measure 80,000 kilometres across – larger than the planet Uranus. #003

The temperature at the centre of the Sun is **150,000 TIMES HOTTER** than boiling water. #004

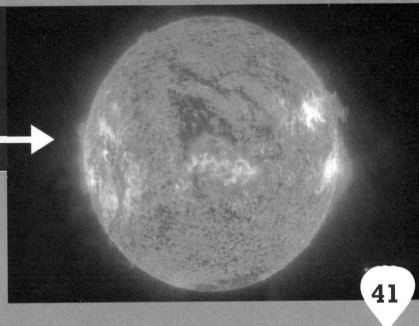

The Sun contains **99.8%** of all the matter in the solar system. #005

10 MIND-BOGGLING MATHS FACTS

If you put a single **grain of rice** on the first square of a chessboard, then two on the next square, then four, and kept on **doubling** the rice, for the last square you would need enough rice to cover India to a depth of 1 metre. #001

The Pirahã tribe in Brazil have words for only 'one', 'two' and 'many' so can't count **three or more objects.** #002

Our system of 60 seconds in a minute and 60 minutes in an hour comes from the **Babylonian counting system** devised 4,000 years ago. #003

$12 + 3 - 4 + 5 + 67 + 8 + 9 = 100$
and
$1 + 2 + 34 - 5 + 67 - 8 + 9 = 100$.
There are at least nine more sums like this. #004

You can turn a strip of paper into a **shape with only one surface** by twisting it once and gluing the ends together. #005

There is an infinite number of infinities. $1, 2, 3...; -1, -2, -3...; 0.1, 0.11, 0.111...; 0.1, 0.12, 0.13...; 0.1, 0.01, 0.001...$ #006

A **googol** is 10^{100}, which is 1 followed by 100 zeroes. This is **larger than any number that needs to be counted.** #007

A **googolplex** is 10^{googol}. It would take longer than the universe has existed (around 13 billion years) to write this number out in full. #008

The pattern of seeds in a sunflower head, the shape of a nautilus seashell and the arrangement of leaves around a plant all follow the same spiral pattern, called the **golden spiral.** #009

The mathematician Descartes invented the system we use for drawing graphs, using X- and Y-axes, after watching a **fly crawl over the ceiling** as he lay in bed. #010

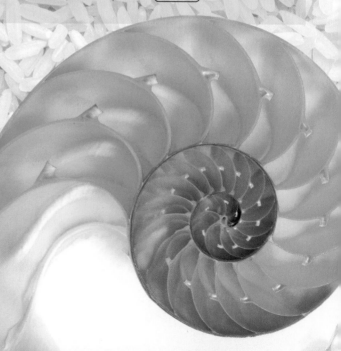

Apollo 11, the spaceflight that took astronauts to the Moon in 1969, had less computing power than a **modern mobile phone.** #001

The Arab inventor al-Jazari made the **first robots** around AD 1200! #002

In the 1830s, Charles Babbage designed the **first computer printer** but it was not built until 2000. #003

3D computer printers **'print' solid objects,** building up the design layer by layer from plastic. #004

The power of computers **doubles** roughly every two years! #005

The **first personal computer**, Altair 8000, was launched in 1975. #006

It had no screen, no keyboard, no disk drive, no mouse and had to be **built from a kit.** #007

45 robots of 14 'species' live in Robotarium X, a **robot zoo** in Portugal. #008

The **first webcam** showed the coffee pot in a university computer lab, to tell workers when the coffee was ready. #009

There are around **17 billion devices** connected to the Internet – more than two for every person on Earth. #010

10 CRAZY COMPUTER FACTS

10 FACTS ON THE HISTORY OF SCIENCE

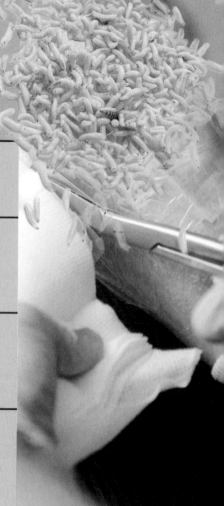

Early doctors put **maggots** into wounds to eat decaying flesh, helping the wounds to heal. #001

The Ancient Greeks thought a camel mating with a leopard produced the **giraffe!** #002

2,600 years ago, Buddhist philosophers suggested that all matter is made of **atoms.** Modern physics has reached the same conclusion. #003

Centuries ago, doctors in India would let an **ant** bite through the edges of a wound then snap off its head, leaving the jaws to act as a stitch. #004

The first important **dinosaur fossils** were found by a 12-year-old girl, Mary Anning, in 1811 in Dorset, England. #005

In 1947, an American engineer invented the **first microwave,** which was nearly 2 metres tall! #006

Scientist Robert Bunsen suffered **partial paralysis** and **lost an eye** in an explosion in 1840 when he was researching toxic and explosive compounds called cacodyls. #007

In 1746, a scientist sent an electric charge along **1,500 metres of wire** held by 200 monks. All the monks yelled at the same time, showing electricity moves very quickly! #008

The **giant squid** was thought to be legendary until it was photographed in 2004. #009

A scientist trying to extract **gold from urine** discovered **phosphorus** by mistake in 1669. #010

Velcro was invented in 1948 after a scientist found burs (sticky seeds) stuck to his dog's fur. (Under a microscope he saw they had tiny hooks.) #001

The **wasabi fire alarm** releases the smell of wasabi, a strong-smelling horseradish, to warn deaf people of fire. #002

Canned food has been around since 1772, but the **can opener** wasn't invented until 1855. #003

In 1996, an American man invented a portable, zip-up cage to hide inside to escape an attack by **killer bees.** #004

In 2007, an American woman invented a bra that converts into two **emergency gas masks.** #005

Sir Francis Bacon invented **frozen chicken** in 1626, but he died from a chill he caught experimenting with his method for freezing the chicken. #006

Barcodes were designed in 1949 by Norman Woodland drawing in sand at the beach. He extended the dots and dashes of Morse code into bands. #007

The **first submarine,** the *Turtle,* used glow-in-the-dark mushrooms to provide light. #008

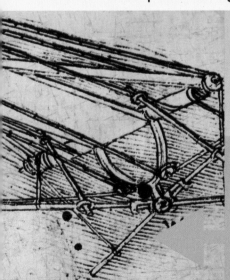

The designers of the **CD** decided it must be able to hold Beethoven's Ninth Symphony at any tempo – so CDs hold **72 minutes of music.** #009

Leonardo da Vinci, who died in 1519, drew designs for a **tank,** a **helicopter,** a **submarine** and a **parachute.** #010

10 EXTREMELY INVENTIVE INVENTIONS

INDEX

ACKNOWLEDGEMENTS

t = top, b = bottom, l = left, r = right, c = centre

Cover images courtesy of istockphoto.com and Shutterstock.com
Back cover bl: Mark Garlick/Getty Images

11 Phil64/Shutterstock.com, 12 Kiev.Victor/Shutterstock.com,
16 JamieRoach/Shutterstock.com, 18 Stanislaw Tokarski/Shutterstock.com,
24 Andy Lidstone/Shutterstock.com, 25 Rob Wilson/Shutterstock.com,
30-31 Stanislav Fosenbauer/Shutterstock.com, 43 Ralph Morse/The LIFE
Picture Collection/Getty Images, 44b Brian J. Skerry/Getty Images